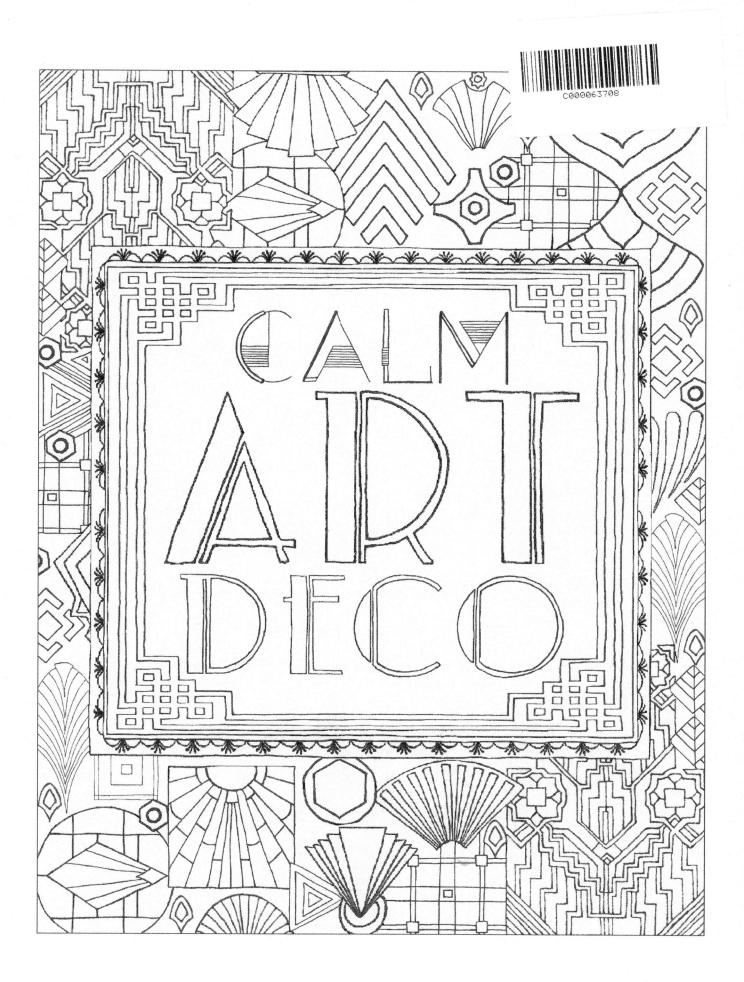

CALM ART DECO

Also by Louisa Banks

Love Paris: Creative Art Therapy for Mindfulness

First published in Great Britain in 2017 by Elmsbury Publishing UK

10 9 8 7 6 5 4 3 2 1

ISBN 978-0-9574878-4-0

Printed in Great Britain

www.elmsbury.com

ELMSBURY

Art Deco is a style that emerged in the mid 1920's,
which influenced the design of buildings, art, jewelry and interiors.
The style represented luxury and modernity and incorporated influences
from several countries (perhaps most notably Egypt).

I hope that the geometric and stylized motifs in this collection provide
a wealth of inspiration to colorists.

The coloring pages in this book are on one side so you can cut out your
finished work if you wish to without ruining anything important
on the reverse.

These pages are suitable for colored pencil, crayon and water based
ink. If you want to try anything heavier I recommend placing a piece
of paper or card underneath the page and using this page
as a test page.

Louisa

Squibb Building New York

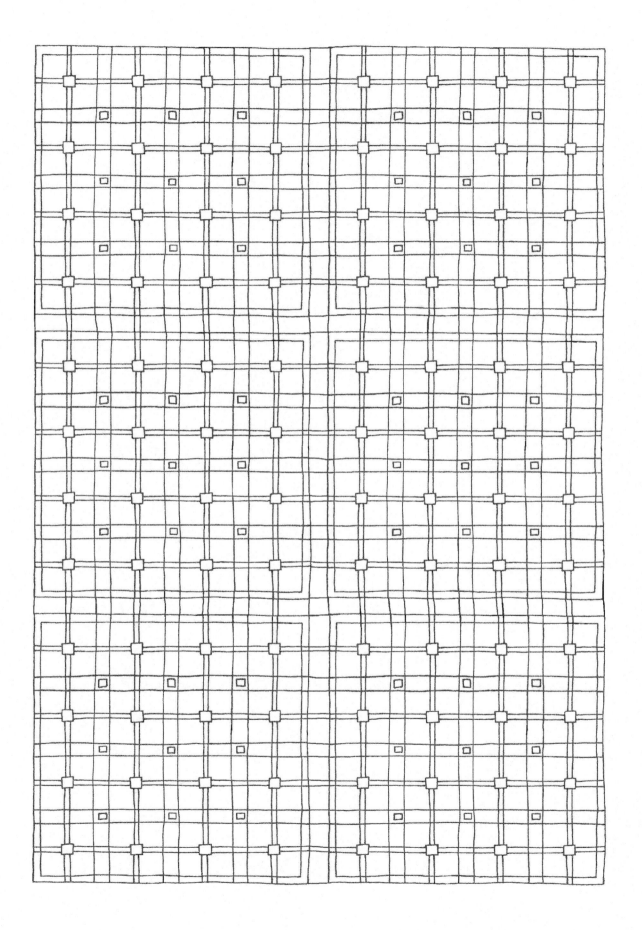

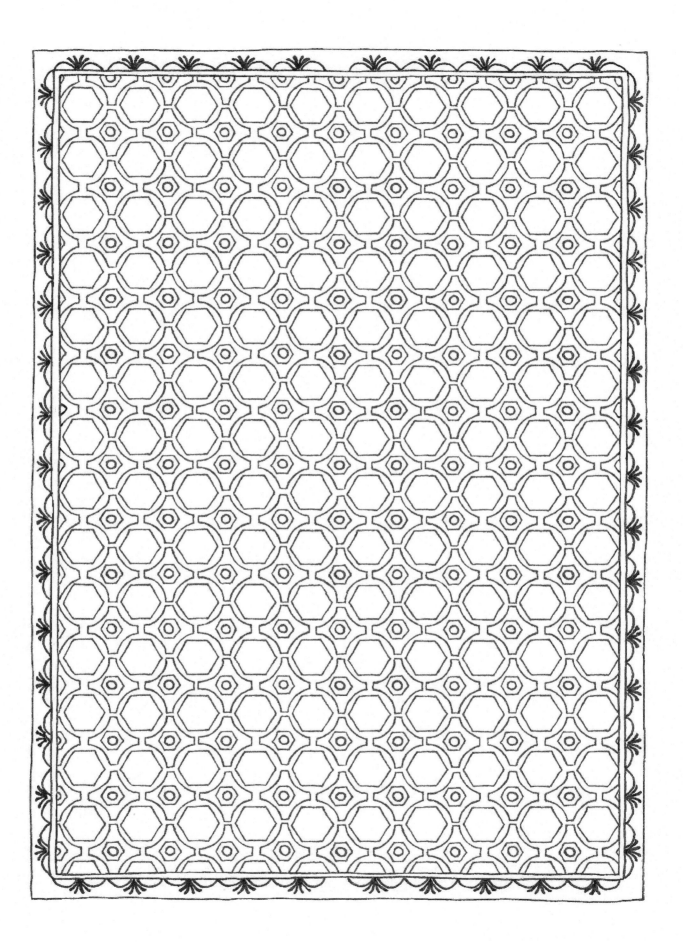

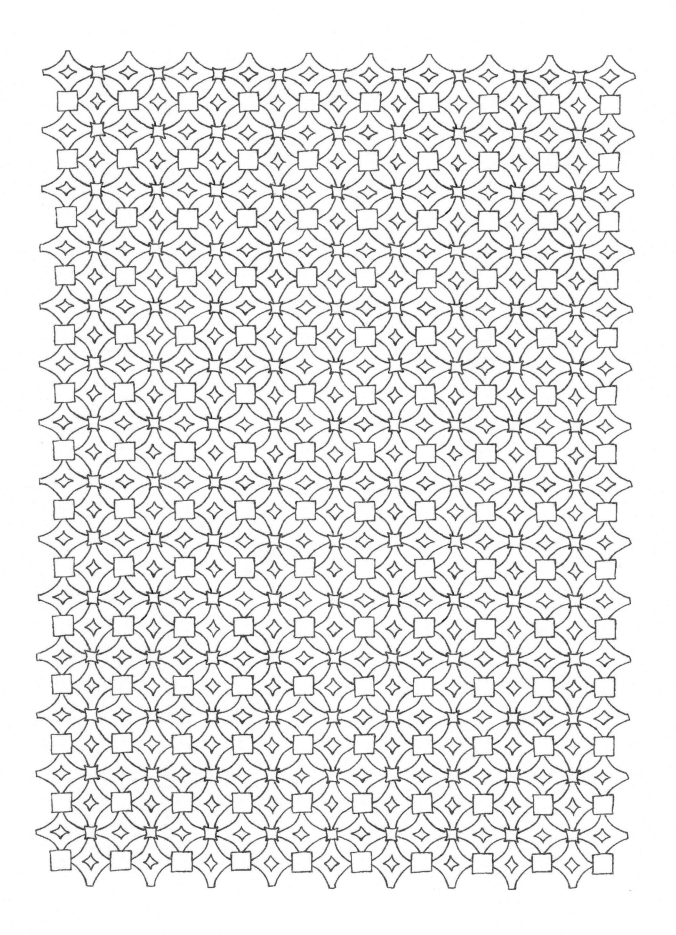

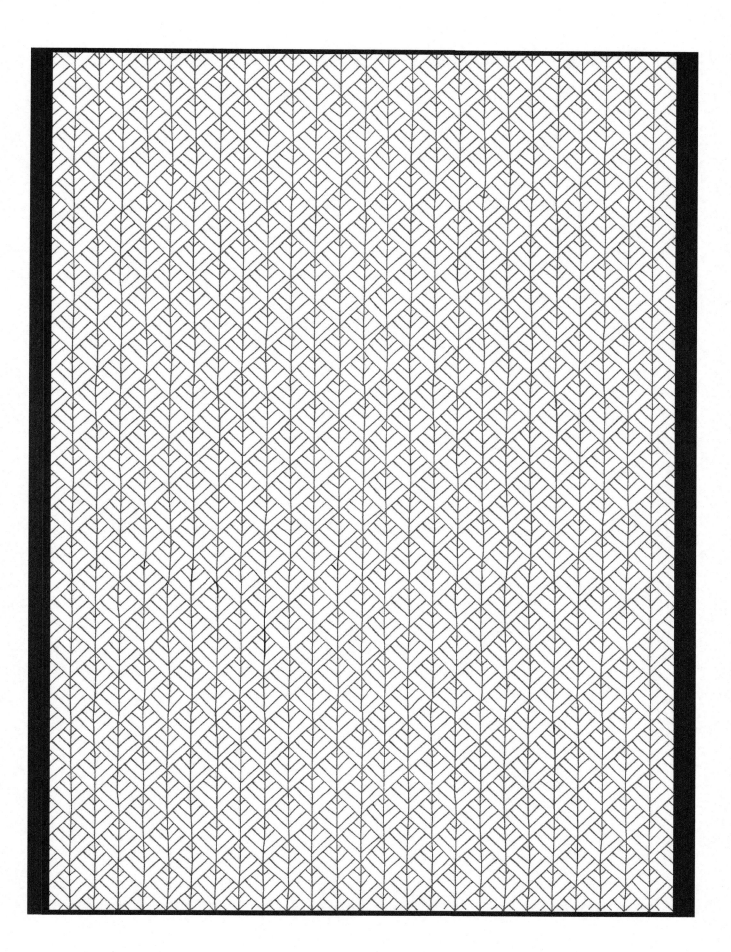

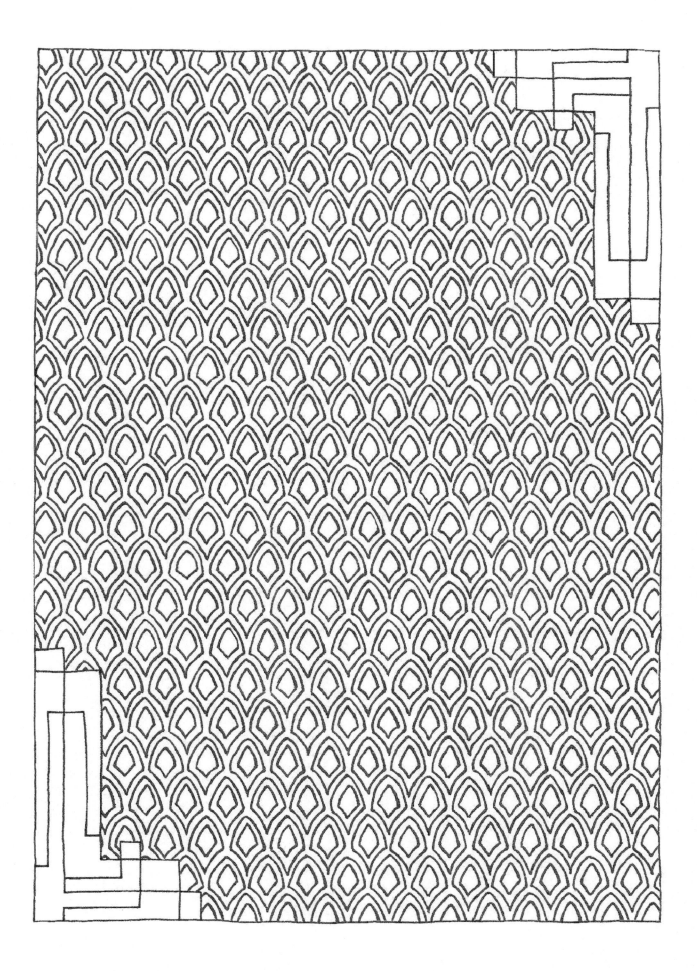

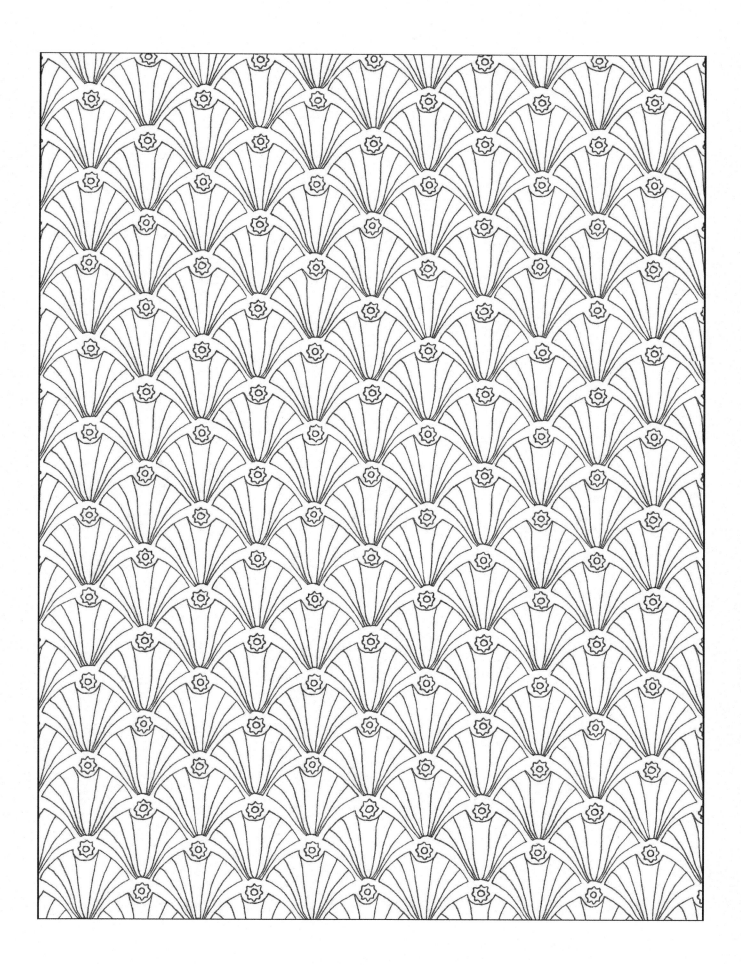

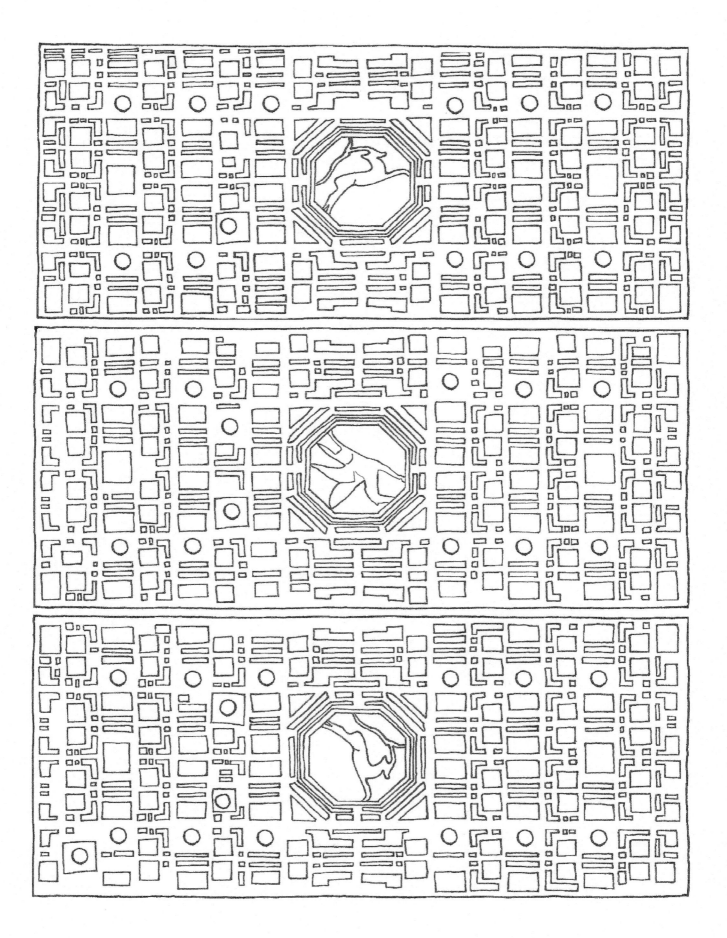

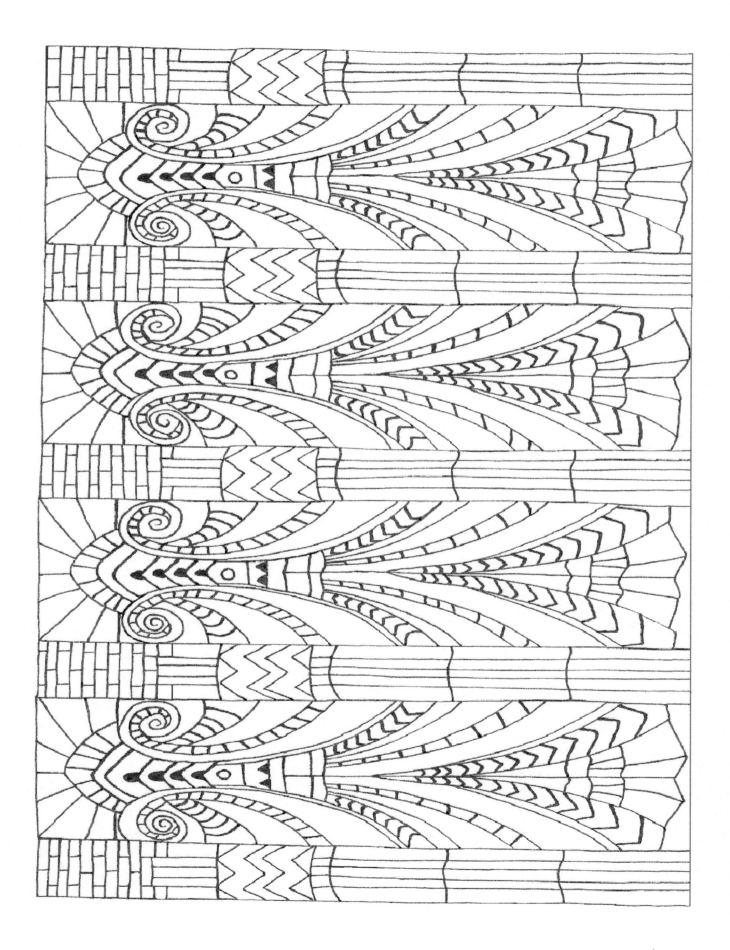